God, Deliver Me From Me

removing the obstacles that keep us stuck

Tina Bailey

CARY, NORTH CAROLINA

Copyright © 2017 by **Tina Bailey**.

All rights reserved. No part of this publication may be reproduced, distributed or transmitted in any form or by any means, including photocopying, recording, or other electronic or mechanical methods, without the prior written permission of the publisher, except in the case of brief quotations embodied in critical reviews and certain other noncommercial uses permitted by copyright law. For permission requests, contact the publisher, addressed "Attention: Permissions Coordinator," at the address below.

Tina Bailey
http://tinabaileyonline.com

Book Cover Design and Layout: Rachel Renee/7 Streams Media

Ordering Information: Quantity sales. Special discounts are available on quantity purchases by corporations, associations, and others. For details, contact the "Special Sales Department" at the address above.

New International Version (NIV)
Holy Bible, New International Version®, NIV® Copyright ©1973, 1978, 1984, 2011 by Biblica, Inc.® Used by permission. All rights reserved worldwide.

English Standard Version (ESV)
The Holy Bible, English Standard Version. ESV® Permanent Text Edition® (2016). Copyright © 2001 by Crossway Bibles, a publishing ministry of Good News Publishers.

New King James Version (NKJV)
Scripture taken from the New King James Version®. Copyright © 1982 by Thomas Nelson. Used by permission. All rights reserved.

God Deliver Me from Me/ Tina Bailey. —1st ed.
ISBN: 978-0-9995265-0-7

CONTENTS

My Wound 1
The Mask 7
Obstacle One: Control 15
Obstacle Two: Comfort 31
Obstacle Three: Fear 45
Surrender 59
About the Author 69

Introduction

We all want the blessings of God and are quick to quote scriptures that show how God has blessings stored up for us, yet we prolong our ability to receive those blessings because we are not living the life God has commanded us to live. It's not until we become honest with ourselves that we can grab hold to the true blessings of God. It's time to get out of the way and allow God to really bless us the way He desires. It's time to stand flatfooted and realize that we are the ones holding up our blessings. It's time to ask God to deliver us from us!

The Bible says that we would not be able to contain all the blessings God has for us (Malachi 3:10). It also says He will give us the desires of our heart (Psalm 37:4). Can you imagine what that would really look like? Can you imagine having so many of your heart's desires that you don't have room enough for them?

Now stop right in your tracks, this is not about materialistic possessions. This is about true blessings from God, those blessings where you can be a blessing to other people. The blessings where you can live a life that mimics the life of Christ, the blessings where your life is the standard of what God is requiring of His people.

In "God, Deliver Me from Me," we will discuss the three obstacles that prevent us from receiving those blessings. We will look at how the issues we hide are rooted in those three obstacles. We will pull those issues up from their root and lay them at God's feet.

This book is written to help you address the areas in your life you need to surrender to God. This is not about judgement from me or anyone else. It is an opportunity for you to get real, surrender, and truly walk in the blessings God has designed for you.

Throughout each section, I have posed questions to help you identify areas in your life to address. These questions will require some deep thought, they will force you to enter places you may have hidden, and they may cause you to realize you haven't healed in areas you thought you had.

I know this to be true because I had to face these things myself. I had to pull down some walls, crawl from under the table, and truly cry out for help. I wasn't pretty but for any wound to heal it must exposed.

My Wound

In my first book, *What You're Hiding is Hindering Your Blessings* I revealed how hiding my feelings and emotions nearly cost me my life. I exposed a lot of pain and anger and truly thought I had dealt with the root of my problems. I was certain the bondage and seclusion that I felt was over. I had called them out. I had revealed them. I wrote a book exposing them.

Yet, I was fooling myself. I was still struggling with my desire to please people, my compulsive binge eating, lying, unfaithfulness, dishonesty, and many other issues I choose not to name.

It wasn't until I got down on my knees and asked God for some real help that I began to see the root of where my problem stemmed. You see I had cried out to God before, but I didn't want to hear His answer. I didn't feel that it was that bad. The things that I was doing weren't that bad. There were things in my life that I didn't feel I had to give up for the blessings of God. I could keep one foot in and one foot out, no one would ever know. But when I realized that my stubbornness, my rebellion, and my selfish desires were hindering me from the true blessings of God, I cried out and said "GOD, DELIVER ME FROM ME!"

When I was finally able to admit that I had a problem with my eating, I turned to a program called Overeaters

Anonymous. It's like Alcoholics Anonymous except it focuses on issues surrounding food and the way we use food as a drug. Well I've never denied the fact that I love food and I have a very strange relationship with it. That acknowledgement should have been reason enough for me to realize I had a problem. Anytime you refuse to let go of something that's killing you, there's something wrong.

In the first meeting, I listened to people talk about their relationship with food and how they realized that without this group, they would be lost and that their addiction to food probably would have killed them in the long run. After about the third "share," I was ready to leave because that was not my problem. I did not feel I needed any program, meal plan, or another human being telling me how to control my eating. I was just fine and I could control my eating if I desired to. So, I left the meeting feeling like they were a bunch of failures and that I didn't need to go back, until one night I found myself sitting in my car stuffing a Little Debbie cake down my throat. When I got home, I had another Little Debbie cake, a bag of pork skins, and a soda as my snack. After eating all that junk, I sat in the middle of my bed and cried out in disgust for consuming over 1500 calories in one sitting. This uncontrollable binging would happen weekly, not because I was hungry but because I was either bored or lonely. Let's give it a name and call it what it was: I was slipping into depression and feeling sorry for myself. Whatever that binge was supposed to help, it DIDN'T! It only made me feel worse.

So back to the commitment of getting it together and gaining control of my eating. I dove into some intensive research, determined to find answers to my problem. I read books, I read articles, and I watched videos and documentaries. I was fixated on finding an answer. I could do this. I was determined to do this. Why was I allowing food to control me?

As I researched my compulsion for eating, I found information about people having a need to control everything and everyone around them. OUCH! That was me. I would find times when not only was I trying to control situations, but when controlling the situation didn't work, I would manipulate the situation to make sure it turned out the way I wanted it to.

I would find myself doing whatever I had to do to make people like me and want to be my friend. I felt that if they didn't want to be my friend there must be something wrong with me. I would get upset with people because they didn't do things the way I wanted them to do them. I would use guilt to make them do things I wanted them to do. I would withhold my affection and love hoping it would make them act the way I wanted them to act. If one person wasn't giving me the attention I wanted, I would go to someone else for a quick fix. Meanwhile, I had no intention of returning the same quality of attention. And when no one was around to manipulate, I would turn to food. I was a mess! On top of being a mess I was lonely and depressed.

It wasn't until I really began to research addictions that I realized I was truly no different from an alcoholic or a drug user. I was addicted to food and control. When I couldn't get my "fix" I was moody and miserable. "God, deliver me from me."

My life was completely out of control. I could no longer make sense of anything in my life. I was paranoid. I felt that no one liked me. I thought people were talking about me. I was having problems making simple decisions because I no longer trusted myself to do the right thing. I found myself constantly looking for validation from people. I just wanted to be found doing the right thing, only I didn't know what that was. My life was out of control and it was getting worse.

I remember sitting down one day to pray. Yes, even during everything I maintained my prayer life. You see, I wanted answers. I just didn't want to meet the requirements needed to receive the answers. Sound familiar?

I remember asking, "Why can't my life be normal?" Then, just as clearly as I had spoken, I heard a response: "BECAUSE YOU DO NOT WANT TO SURRENDER!"

That was real. Have you asked God to take control of your situation but you just don't want to surrender it? You go to the altar, cry out to God to help you, and after you wipe your tears, you pick the problem up and take it back to your seat with you.

I had to figure out a way to get rid of this wound once and for all. What exactly did God want me to surrender and why was I determined to hold on to it?

What wound are you covering up? Look deep! Are you holding on to a behavior that God has pressed on your heart to let go, yet instead of letting it go, you hide it with another destructive behavior? Write about it.

The Mask

Even though we celebrated most holidays growing up, we never went all out for Halloween. We either went to church for what was called "Hallelujah Night" where we dressed like Biblical Characters, played games, and the adults passed out candy, or we went around to the neighbors' houses (who were family members) and they gave us candy. Either way it was a very controlled and safe atmosphere. Unlike today, we never had to worry about people giving us candy laced with drugs or hiding needles inside. You also knew which candy came from which house because you only went to a few houses.

Dressing up was simple: it was merely a costume from the local retail store with a plastic mask or something my mom made with an old sheet. It was nothing extravagant.

Well today, we walk around as if every day is Halloween and we have these extravagant costumes. We have worn our costumes for so long, they have become a part of our reality.

I remember seeing this post on social media where there was a demon putting on a costume of a Christian and the caption said, "It's time to get ready to go to church." At first glance it was funny, but then as I thought about it, we do this every day. We put on a costume every day hoping no one will see who we really are.

The mask we wear has been custom made to fit us perfectly. Sadly, some of us have different masks for different occasions. We have a mask for church, a mask for work, a mask for when we are hanging out with our friends, and we even have a mask we put on in our own homes. Yet we wonder why we don't know what we want in life or what we are called to do. We've hidden behind a mask for so long the real person has become lost and unproductive.

Do you find yourself acting differently around certain people or in certain environments? Have you lost contact with the person you were created to be? Do you find yourself grasping at opportunities only to leave them incomplete? Maybe you just want to get back to that place where you felt happy but you don't remember how. It's been so long.

What does your mask look like? Where do find yourself wearing your mask? Have you become comfortable in your mask? Is it your reality? I've asked a lot of questions. Write the answers to these questions and how those answers make you feel.

_____
_____
_____
_____
_____
_____
_____

Breathe! Breathe deep! You are no different from anyone else. We all wear a mask at some point. The problem is when we get lost in those fake images and lose sight of who we really are.

I remember one year my mother purchased a Wonder Woman costume for me. The costume itself was made of this thick plastic and because I was "big for my age," it didn't fit quite right. To accommodate this mishap, my brother took a sheet and tied it around my neck like a cape. I put one of my mother's bracelets on each wrist, popped on the mask and out the door I trotted. For that night, I had super powers. I was strong and could accomplish anything. I remember running up the street so my cape could blow in the wind. I was everything until it got hot under that mask and I began to sweat. I wanted to take the mask off but my brother told me I would lose my super hero powers if I did. So of course, I kept the mask on until it was time to go in for the night. I didn't know it then, but I was setting myself up to believe I could never have "super hero powers" as myself. I really do believe that was the beginning of some of my self-esteem issues.

I always wanted to be someone else. I wanted to be smaller. I wanted to be taller. I wanted to be smarter. I wanted to be whiter. I wanted to be anyone but who I was.

Did you ever want to take off the mask but felt people would not accept the person you revealed? People had become accustomed to the imaginary you and you just weren't sure if they would accept who you really were? Maybe you wouldn't accept the person under the mask.

Whether you call it a wound or a mask, God wants you to LET IT GO! He desires to have all of you. The real you.

The hurts. The struggles. The pains. The parts that others talk about. The parts that you try to hide. The parts that disgust you. The parts that make you cry when you think about them. The parts you wish weren't there. He wants all of them. Every part of you.

The decisions you made that led down a path of regret, He knows about them. The relationship you tried to hide, He knows about it. The lies and manipulation, He knows about them. The addictions, He knows about them. The hurt and bitterness, He knows. The tears you cry every night, He sees them. The loneliness you feel, He wants to fulfill it. He loves you and wants to use you for His glory! He just wants you to surrender to Him.

What appears to be a hindrance in surrendering to God can be summed up by three obstacles:

Control

Frustration over our inability to control a situation or our determination to be in control of a situation.

Comfort

We grow comfortable in a situation or circumstance.

Fear

Our fears keep us bound and chained to a situation or circumstance.

Regardless which category of obstacle your wound or what you are hiding behind your mask falls under, God can help you overcome it if you are willing to allow Him. If you are ready, let's go. Let's do the work together.

Obstacle One: Control

According to Oxford Press, "Control is the power to influence or direct a person's behavior or course of events." I define control as, using your power or influence to manipulate people, opportunities, and emotions to have your way.

Control is one of those issues that's easy to hide behind a mask because if you are good at it, no one will ever know they are being controlled. I will admit, I was good at it, very good at it. I can look back now and realize there were situations I was controlling and no one was aware of the control including myself. I also look at those moments and see those were times I felt the most out of control.

Many of the situations I found myself in were because I wanted to be in control. I wanted things my way and was willing to manipulate and be compromised to have it my way. Control showed up in my life several different ways. It showed up in my eating disorder, people pleasing, abusive relationships, anger, pity, manipulation, low self-esteem, OCD behaviors, perfectionism, and even in my fears. Control can be a monster if you don't surrender it.

It took me years to admit I had a control issue. I was either attempting to control others or allowing their actions to control me. Because this book is about you, we will not seek to blame others for your issues. We will address them as they are and be upfront about them.

Admitting your allowance of the mistreatment of others and their negative behaviors as a means of you controlling a situation is hard but vital to your surrender. It's easy to blame everyone else for your feelings, hurt and pain, yet hard to admit you allowed those behaviors for personal gain. Truth is, we can stop any behavior if we desire to. Disclaimer: I'm not talking about moments of attack like rape. I'm talking about long-term behaviors and actions you are exposed to that are consistent and unchanging.

Any behavioral study will tell you, true recovery begins when you admit you have a problem. You cannot surrender and hold on at the same time. It won't work.

What areas in your life have you tried to control?

_____
_____
_____
_____
_____
_____
_____
_____

How did controlling those situations serve you?

_____
_____
_____
_____
_____

I may need them

We have a tendency of holding on to things "just in case we need them" someday. For years I held on to a pair of pants, hoping to be able to get back into them. Each season I would try on those pants, neatly fold them up and place them back in the bin. Each year I would say I'll be in them next year. Each time I moved to another house, they took the trip with me. I held onto those pants for at least fifteen years before I finally threw them away. As I thought about things that prevent us from walking in our purpose and surrendering to God, He reminded me of those pants.

Those pants were my connection to the past. Those pants were my hope of things from the past. Those pants were there just in case I needed them later. Those pants were a reminder of the potential and a blindfold to reality. Truth is, those pants were my way of controlling my thoughts. I was manipulating the situation to get what I wanted and what I desired. I wanted to lose weight and the pants were supposed to be my motivation to do so. Well at least I could tell myself that, right?

Those pants were a constant reminder of the way things were in my life: unfulfilling, depressing, and useless. They were a constant reminder of my past and how I longed for the return of feelings of fulfillment, excitement, and happiness. They were no longer my reality. Each time I tried on those pants, I was reminded of how much weight I had gained. The act of trying on those pants initiated an emotional pain that triggered other pains in my life. Those pants drew out feelings of abandonment, defeat, shame, and guilt. They reminded me of the way I desired things to be yet was unable to obtain. They kept me grasping for hope that one day my reality would fade into my fantasy.

Just like I held onto those pants, we hold on to other circumstances and painful events the same way. We grab hold with complete belief that things will change. We hold on so tight and so long that we forget just how much holding on is hurting us. We keep it near just in case the situation changes. We keep it near just in case we need it later.

When you hold on to things that no longer serve you, it is a form of control. You are hoping the feelings associated with whatever you are holding to will eventually give you the outcome you desire. When your feelings aren't moved by the circumstance, you blame the circumstance instead of looking at the reality and changing the reality. Sometimes we want the desired outcome so bad, we are willing to hurt ourselves and those around us to have it.

The pants didn't change sizes over the years. They were the same size then as they were when I purchased them. They didn't change, I did. My reality changed. But I was determined to hold on to the past. I longed for the fantasy.

What you are holding on to in hopes that one day it will change?

_____
_____
_____
_____
_____
_____
_____

Maybe it's a bad relationship. Maybe it's a job that no longer fulfills your needs. Maybe it's a friendship that has ran its course. Maybe it's a behavior you wish you could stop. Whatever you are holding on to, ask yourself, "Am I holding on in hopes the situation will change?" If the answer to your question is yes, you are using that situation to control an outcome. Here's the thing; you cannot control other people, circumstances, or situations. In many instances, you cannot even control yourself. All you can control is how you interpret the situation and how you intend to adjust to it.

Look back at your list. Why are you holding on? What do you desire to get out of holding onto the person, circumstance, or situation?

_____
_____

_____
_____
_____
_____
_____
_____

God don't care!

Have you ever felt your problem was too much for God? You wanted to surrender and cry out to God but felt "I've messed up too bad this time, God will never forgive me for this." We feel we need to clean ourselves up before we can go to God. We feel He could never forgive us for that. Or maybe He'll forgive us but at what cost? Surely the punishment will be severe.

In Jeremiah 33, the Bible declares there is nothing new under the sun. Anything you find yourself going through, trust and believe someone else has already went through it or something similar. You can also believe that God faithfully brought them out of it and He will bring you out as well… IF you allow Him and if you relinquish your need to control the outcome.

It really doesn't matter how big, how dirty, or how nasty your situation is, God is not like man. He will never turn His nose up at you or judge you for your sin. He loves you more than anything on this earth. Think about it like this, if God is concerned about the sparrow and provides for it every day, don't you think He would be just as concerned or more concerned about you? Aren't you worth more than a bird? (Matthew 6:25-26)

The Bible says we are to cast all our cares on Him (God) because He cares for us. (1 Peter 5:7) That scripture did not say cast the small things on Him. It does not say cast the things that are easy. It does not say cast some of our cares. It says cast ALL our cares on Him. The problem is we want to come to God as a last resort. We only want to give God the things that we feel we cannot handle. CONTROL! Then we still maintain a hold on them when we "give them over." MORE CONTROL! Maybe we even feel our situations are small and God doesn't have time to deal with such small issues. Anything that concerns us, concerns God!

Think about that area in your life you believe is too small or too big to "bother" God with. Isn't it time to hand it over? What's holding you back? Why do you think God isn't concerned with it? What in your past has brought you to this decision?

_____
_____
_____
_____
_____
_____
_____
_____
_____

Control or Independence

My desire to be in control started at an early age. I just didn't know it was control. Until I became honest with myself, I called it independence. I was not controlling, I was merely independent. Capable of doing for myself without help from anyone.

Earlier I gave a definition of control as using your power or influence to manipulate people, opportunities, and emotions to have your way. My definition for independence is a conscious decision to live in a way free of a person's control or authority over you.

Regardless of how you look at it, the intent is to control the outcome of the situation by taking authority over it. Control is independence with an attitude.

As the baby of the family and the only girl, I was quite spoiled, bossy, and manipulative. I was very strong-willed and didn't like to ask for help. My grandmother would say, "she's so independent" and I ran with that idea. Truth is, it was more than independence; I was controlling and wanted things my way.

Just like me, for many the seed of control was planted at an early age and labeled independence. We teach our children to tie their shoes, put on their clothes, clean up behind themselves, feed themselves, and bathe themselves. However, do we teach them to ask for help when they need it?

My mother's favorite line when I was growing up was, "handle your business," her way of teaching me to take care of myself. In fact, many times I was told, "do for yourself because no one else will." I used this insight as motivation for some of my best manipulation performances. I had to do for myself because no one else would. I had to take control of the situation, because I was the only one that could handle it.

There is nothing wrong with taking care of yourself. In fact, it is very healthy to be able to tend to your own needs. But don't allow your independence to slip into a need to control everything and everyone around you. Even the most independent person needs help at some point.

I didn't know it was okay to be independent and ask for help. Asking for help will never take away from your independence. It means you are growing and independence comes with growth. It means you are doing bigger things. Most people don't ask for help on things they have mastered. They ask for help when something is new or they can't get over the hump.

When a person has been conditioned to be independent or "handle their own business," it's difficult for them to depend on anyone including God.

We see our need to ask for help as a challenge to our independence and a means of giving away our control. There is no one greater to give your control to than God.

When I gave away my desire to be in control, my world seemed easier to handle. The burden of doing everything myself was lifted. I never knew how heavy control was. Its weight was far more than I was ever created to bear, far more than I desired to bear.

Do you feel it shows a lack of character or discipline to ask for help? Is it a sign of weakness to not be able to handle a situation? For a long time, I thought crying showed weakness. I thought asking for help was a sign that I wasn't good enough. Not because someone told me that but because I felt I should be able to handle it. There were times I felt inadequate if I had to take an issue before God. I no longer considered myself a babe in Christ, so I should be able to handle the "easy" situations, right? Instead of bringing the concern to God, I would hold onto it until it became a big issue, I was in over my head and could no longer manipulate the situation to get the desired result. Anytime you place "should" in front of a statement or phrase – is a clear sign you are seeking control.

What areas have you labeled as independence but are able to see now as a means of control?

_____
_____
_____
_____
_____

Maybe your desire wasn't about control. Could it have been your desire to prove to others that you could handle the situation? Was there an expectation or the lack of an expectation of your ability? What do you feel a need to prove?

_____
_____
_____
_____

Is that same feeling preventing you from asking God for help? What feelings does asking for help bring up in you?

_____
_____
_____
_____
_____
_____

God is faithful and capable of handling all our issues. It amazes me that He cares about what is bothering me, what bothers you, what bothers the person laying on the side of the street, even the person who has decided not to have a relationship with Him at all. Our concerns matter. What an amazing God Who would take the time to care about my issues. Yet I held on to problems and concerns because I didn't feel He cared about them. That's not true. I held on to those problems and concerns because I wanted to change them. I wanted to be in control of them. I wanted things to turn out my way. I wanted Him to fix them, my way.

Did you ever have the idea that a problem was too big for God or that He didn't care about your issue? Could it have been from your childhood? Did you have a problem and you took it to the person you felt should be able to help you and they made you feel like it was all your fault? Perhaps they didn't console you the way you felt you should be consoled. Were you expecting a solution to the problem but they couldn't provide one for you so you found yourself having to figure it out for yourself? Did you ever hear the actual words, "Oh that's out of my realm, I can't help you with that"?

Maybe it wasn't your childhood years, maybe this thought occurred as an adult. You've turned to others for help and they couldn't or wouldn't help you. Did you reach out for help and your cries went unheard? Let's be real: have you cried out to God but didn't hear the answer you wanted to hear? Or maybe He wasn't acting fast enough? In the book of Isaiah Chapter 55 verse 8, the Lord declares, "For my thoughts are not your thoughts, neither are your ways my ways." God may not respond to you the way you desire. He may not respond when you want Him to respond. But I love the fact that scripture tells us to be confident in approaching God because if we ask anything according to His will, He hears us (1 John 5:14). And then in Isaiah it says, before they call I will answer, while they are still speaking I will hear. (65:24).

Think about that for a moment. Before you even finish asking God for an answer, He is already working it out. You may be saying, that sounds good but why doesn't it feel like it? Have you really surrendered it to Him or are you afraid that it will be too big or too much for Him to handle? Are you afraid you will have to give up your control over the situation?

There was a young lady whose mother loved vintage jewelry. Her mother had fallen ill and the young lady wanted to do something to show her mother how much she loved her. She went to several vintage shops looking for the perfect piece of jewelry. As she traveled, she found several exquisite pieces but decided against purchasing anything. When asked why, she replied, "My mom is fragile and those pieces were too heavy." She traveled all around the world looking for the perfect piece of jewelry. Soon her brother called to inform her that her mother had passed away. The young lady was distraught. She had wasted time looking for the perfect piece of jewelry, worrying about its size instead of spending time with her mother. When she returned home she noticed that her mother had left her a package. Inside the package was a pendant the young lady had passed over several months ago. The jeweler knew the daughter really liked the pendant and sent it to her mother's home. The mother opened the package and immediately fell in love with the piece. Before dying she placed the pendent in its original package and left a note for her daughter. The note read, "I loved the pendant. It reminded me of the one I wanted to purchase for my mom many years ago but felt it was more than she could handle in her fragile state. Thank you for trusting my ability to handle such a wonderful piece."

So many times, we carry burdens around with us because we feel God cannot handle them, they are too big or too small to take to Him, or we've made up in our minds we can handle it. All He wants is for us to trust Him enough to give it to Him, but this is hard to do when you desire to be in control.

Are you ready to deal with your need to be in control? Could your control be the glue holding your mask in place?

PRAYER

God,

Thank You for providing me an opportunity to identify my truth and to be honest with myself and You concerning my need to control. I realize I am not equipped to handle the situations that occur in my life without Your help. I also realize my need to be in control has placed a barrier between us. Help me to let go of my controlling behaviors. Help me to move past my desire to have things my way. Help me to turn to You first instead of as a last resort. Forgive me for attempting to handle this on my own. I trust you with my life and with my need to control. In Jesus name, I pray.

****

As I asked God to deliver me from a desire and need to be in control, I found it necessary to submerge myself in His Word. Below are some scriptures and affirmations that helped along the way. I believe they will do the same for you. Repeat them daily as needed.

SCRIPTURES

Many are the plans in the mind of a man, but it is the purpose of the Lord that will stand. Proverbs 19:21 (ESV)

Therefore, do not be anxious about tomorrow, for tomorrow will be anxious for itself. Sufficient for the day is its own trouble. Matthew 6:34 (ESV)

Do not be anxious about anything, but in everything by prayer and supplication with thanksgiving let your requests be made known to God. And the peace of God, which surpasses all understanding, will guard your hearts and your minds in Christ Jesus. Philippians 4:6-7 (ESV)

Whatever the Lord pleases, he does, in heaven and on earth, in the seas and all deeps. Psalm 135:6 (ESV)

Jesus answered him, "What I am doing you do not understand now, but afterward you will understand." John 13:7 (ESV)

The Lord shows us how we should live, and he is pleased when he sees people living that way. Psalm 37:23 (ERV)

But he said to me, "My grace is sufficient for you, for my power is made perfect in weakness." Therefore, I will boast all the more gladly of my weaknesses, so that the power of Christ may rest upon me." 2 Corinthians 12:9 (ESV)

AFFIRMATIONS

I am relaxed and calm. My thoughts are under God's control.

I let go of all expectations and allow God to lead me in the direction He desires.

I leave my past in the past and allow God to lead me into my future.

I choose freedom over my desire to be in control.

I find true peace when I give my desires over to God and His will.

Obstacle Two: Comfort

Imagine taking a nice hot bath after a long day full of activity. As you sit in the tub, you look forward to settling into your bed without interruption. You mentally go over your plans for tomorrow and realize you don't have any activities until afternoon. You feel every muscle in your body relax and enjoy the warmth of the water and the thought of sleeping in. You get into bed and soon find yourself pulling the covers up over your body, continuing to find comfort in not having to be responsible for anything for several hours. You take a deep breath and before you know it, the alarm goes off and you are startled out of your sleep. The comfort you anticipated was interrupted and now you are required to make a change. That's exactly what happens when we are called to make a change and life has become comfortable and even predictable.

When life becomes comfortable, we tend to reject anything that resembles change. We are creatures of habit. We become comfortable in our habits and find them hard to let go. Whether they are habits we learned as a child or habits we picked up as an adult, we embrace them. They become a part of our routine. They become a part of our lives. We plan our days and our activities around them.

We even surround ourselves with others that have the same habits so that we won't have to change them.

Making changes to our routines and changing our habits is uncomfortable. Even when we want to let go of the pain and hurt that surround our lives, we hold on because it's comfortable. We know what to expect from the pain. It has been a part of our lives for years. We know how to cover up the hurt. Whether it is with lies, excuses, or by hurting others, we can mask the hurt until it becomes tolerable. We hold on to pain like it is the ticket to life. We find ourselves struggling with the idea of, "if I let go of the pain, I don't know what else to hold on to." Have you tried PEACE? Have you tried FREEDOM? How about JOY? Any of those would allow you to feel better physically and emotionally.

Where do you find comfort? What habits do you have that you've become comfortable with?

_____

_____

_____

_____

_____

I'm good with my Comfort

I remember when I first started re-focusing on my health, determined to lose weight for once and for all. I was tired of observing myself sitting in front of the television watching some weight-loss reality show while eating chips and snack cakes, thinking I'll start tomorrow. The truth is, I knew tomorrow would never come. I knew I had to decide on a day and make that the day this would change.

The first thing I had to do was to be honest with myself. I wasn't tired enough. Even though walking up a flight of stairs made me winded, I had become comfortable in my fat suit. I knew what to expect or what not to expect. I knew what would work and what would not work. I had become used to the fat suit. In all honesty, I didn't see myself as fat every day. You know how on those days when your clothes fit and you think you're cute, you don't feel fat? But whoa to those days when the only thing left in your closet to wear are the clothes that are too tight and show every bulge on your body. Those are the days you don't feel fat, you feel like the elephant that ate the hippo.

I had become used to people looking at me a certain way when I walked into the room. I had accepted that there were just some outfits I would not be able to wear. I knew there were some places I just would not be able to go. I knew that traveling would be just a little different for me, whether it was an extended seatbelt or maybe an extra stop to stretch my legs. All those things had become comfortable. They were the norm. But now you want me to change that?

You want me to start watching what I eat? You want me to walk up the stairs instead of using the elevator? You want me to prepare my meals every day instead of stopping and grabbing something on the way? That's not what I'm used to doing. Those things are outside of my comfort zone. I don't know how those things are going to feel. I want the changes but I don't want to be uncomfortable. I want the outcome but I don't want to do what it takes to get it. It is uncomfortable.

Okay so maybe your problem isn't your weight. Have you become comfortable in your relationship? You know the one that everyone warned you about? The one that has you on an emotional roller coaster. One day things seem to be going good; the communication is great and you seem to be able to finish each other's sentences. You seem to be on the same page and things are wonderful. But then there are those days when everything you say is taken out of context. You assume things that haven't been spoken. Regardless of what the intent was, the outcome is so far from what you expected it to be. There are more arguments than moments of laughter. It just never seems to be enough.

You realize it's time to make a change. The alternative to what is already there is walking away from what you have become used to. You begin to justify your comfortable discomfort. The arguments aren't really that bad. You say, "We just need to work on our lines of communication. We are just going through a bad patch, it will get better." You dismiss the fact that the bad patch has been going on for years. The idea of starting over or finding someone else to date is overwhelming. You think to yourself, "at least I'm with someone and we have fun sometimes. If I walk away, I may be lonely. I've never been by myself before, what will that feel like?"

Maybe you can't relate to either of those situations. Here is another scenario to consider. You know there is a calling on your life yet you are afraid to answer it because you don't know what will be required of you. You may not be called to enter the pulpit but there is a burden growing inside of you to help people. What are you going to have to give up to answer this calling? What will it feel like? What will you really have to do? What will you have to change about your current life? What if they don't receive you? What do you have to offer? Those are all comfort zone questions.

If God has called you to do His work, He is faithful to provide you with the tools to accomplish every goal He places before you. Let's be real. The issue is not the calling. The issue is that you do not want to give up your comfort level. It is that you do not want to have to grow into something different. You have become comfortable and you don't want to make the necessary changes.

So many times, God has given us instructions or called us to move to another level of growth and we fight it. It's not because we do not understand the instructions. It's not because we don't have the abilities required to go to the next level but because we don't want to give up our comfort zone.

Do you feel the nagging inside to make a change, yet you struggle with what it will feel like? What will be expected of you? You know you need to step out in faith but who will catch you? What has staying in your comfort zone prevented you from accomplishing?

_____
_____
_____

Why Should I Move Comfort?

Regardless of which scenario you relate to, you will never grow into the real blessings of God until you move away from your comfort zone. The comfort zone is designed to keep you from the abundance created for you. Refusing to make changes in your health, settling in toxic relationships, or being afraid to answer God's call on your life are symptoms associated with being in a comfort zone. You are missing out on the true blessings of God because of your comfort.

God will never push you. He will never make you do anything you do not want to do. But you cannot be upset when you don't receive the blessings you have been asking for when you are unwilling to make the sacrifices required for those blessings.

You must understand that surrendering to God and His plans require change. You cannot remain in your comfort zone and surrender to God. It may be that God requires you to change your environment. He may require that you change the people in your circle. He may even require that you seclude yourself from everyone. Are you willing to make that change? Are you willing to step out of your comfort zone and answer the call? Are you willing to do whatever it takes?

Many times, we become so comfortable with our situation that we don't want to let go until we absolutely must. The thing is by that time, so much damage has been done. Now not only do we have to deal with the situation, we also must deal with the path of destruction our comfort has made.

I remember having a pair of shoes. I loved those shoes. There were black and I could wear them with anything. They were flats so I could dress them up or wear them casually. They were comfortable. I wore those shoes until they had a hole in the bottom of them. Sadly, even with the hole in them, I continued to wear them until one day I got caught in the rain. I quickly realized that a hole in the sole of your shoe and a water puddle don't match. The puddle will win every time.

Don't get so comfortable with your situation that you miss your blessing because of your unwillingness to let go of the comfort.

God has so many blessings that He wants to release to us. I really don't believe we can wrap our minds around what He has for us. But how can He give us anything when we walk around with a mediocre mindset, a willingness to accept the minimum, a lack of desire to pursue the abundance, or an inability to sacrifice comfort for the miraculous?

Imagine having the ability and the intent to be a blessing to someone. You realize the person needs the help. You are ready to provide that need. All you need is for the person to ask for your help. But because the person isn't comfortable asking for help they miss out on their blessing. Imagine you have intended to give the person $100 but they only ask for $10. Although you can give more and you intended to give more, they only asked for the minimum. Because they were willing to settle for the minimum and because they were comfortable with less than what was available, they walked away with only the minimum.

Are you walking away with only the minimum from God because you are too comfortable in your current situation to ask Him for the abundance? Have you become so comfortable in your situation that you don't expect more? Are you afraid of moving out of your comfort zone because you don't know what the alternative will look like? Maybe you aren't moving out of your comfort zone because you don't know how.

We sit around making declarations about what WE want God to do. WE make plans. WE set goals. Yet we never take the time to ask God what He desire our next step to be. I guarantee if you would take a moment to inquire of His plan, things would go a lot smoother for you.

In the midst of making all our plans, we fail to put action with our words, then we get mad when God doesn't move the way we expected Him to move. Did you ever stop to think He was waiting for you? God is not a genie in a bottle. You don't rub Him, tell Him what you want and it magically appears. You must put in some work. You must make some moves. Sometimes those moves require you to let go of what you are used to and step into the unknown. But that's what surrendering to God is: stepping into the unknown, stepping out of what is comfortable and predictable.

How Do I Move?

Moving out of your comfort zone can be difficult. Most of our comforts are the result of habits that we have formed over the years. Those habits are attached to some type of success. For example, each morning we get up, brush our teeth, and go about our day. We don't think about all the steps required in brushing our teeth. We just do it. Then we go to the dentist and our reward for faithfully brushing our teeth every day is no cavities.

One of the areas I settled in on was my controlling behavior. You can replace where I've put control with the area you would like God to deliver you from.

Once I made up my mind to surrender my controlling behaviors, my world changed. The people in my corner of life were conditioned by my controlling tendencies and depended on them. When I asked God to release me of those tendencies, it required me AND them to make some hard adjustments. They didn't like me controlling their lives, but they had become accustomed to it. In order for me to walk in my deliverance, I had to give them back their lives. So, when I gave back their lives, it required them to learn how to handle certain issues that arose in their life. Honestly, it required them to handle all the issues that arose in their life. They were bitter because now they were forced out of their own comfort zone. Beware: you may have to deal with some backlash of stepping out of your comfort zone, but it is okay. You are doing this for you. You are making this change for you. The people in your circle may not realize it yet, but they will reap the benefit in the long run.

As I walked out of my comfort zone, it allowed the people around me to grow. They became stronger. They stepped out of their own comfort zones and did things they didn't realize they were capable of doing. They learned new habits and behaviors. They began to trust themselves in their own affairs.

Stepping out of my comfort zone was not easy. There are still areas that I'm working on. I ask you to seek God to discover any comfort zones in your life that are interfering with your potential. He will meet you there and will give instructions on how to step out of the comfort if you allow Him to guide you.

Here are some suggestions to get you started.

1. Admit you have settled into a comfort zone. Admittance is the first step in changing any behavior. As I said it took me years to admit I had a problem. There are still areas in my life that I surrender to God every day. It is an on-going surrender. It will not happen overnight and it will not end immediately. But what I love most about God is all He requires is your willingness to want to change and He handles the rest.

2. Change your habits. Walk outside of the box. If when your children come to you with a problem and you are quick to give a solution, stop and ask them how they can fix the issue. A lot of times we are quick to help someone else fix their issues because we don't want to deal with our own. Their issues are always easy to fix and it takes our mind off our own for a few minutes. Your issues will

still be waiting for you when you finish solving theirs.

3. Work on yourself. Earlier you wrote down areas in your life where you struggled with control and comfort. Examine them. What can you do to change the habits associated with them? What can you do to identify the triggers associated with them? Why do you feel a need to hold on to them? What are they hiding? Now is the time to focus your attention on your own issues. You freed yourself from the issues of others, now work on you.

4. Start small. One thing I learned the hard way is you don't want to drop everything at one time. You can't go from being in complete control of everything and everyone to one day not doing anything for anyone. You will land in a place of isolation and depression. Your body and mind were content with handling the issues of others. You were happy with avoiding your own issues. Jumping in head first with your own issues can be overwhelming. Pace yourself and be patient! You have the rest of your life to deal with your issues. One step at a time wins the race.

5. Do something every day to build your trust in yourself. Most people who have issues letting go tend to struggle with making decisions that relate to them. It's easier to tell others what they need but

the smallest choices related to self-advancement can wreak havoc on the mind of a control freak. Yes, I called you a control freak! Guess what? I am too!

6. Find a new hobby. Find something to fill your time. You have spent years controlling the lives of your loved ones. You need to find something to fill that time with. When you find yourself slipping into past behaviors, this hobby will provide an outlet for that energy and attention.

It will take time. Be patient with yourself. Give it to God. Remember He is concerned about what you are concerned about. He wants to help you. He desires to help you. He loves helping you.

PRAYER

God,
Deliver me from my desire to stay in my comfort zone. I realize I can never grow to who or what You created me to be if I reside in this place of comfort. God, when I feel I cannot continue, help me to lean on You for strength. When searching for Your strength seems impossible or I just can't feel Your presence, I will remember the sacrifice of comfort Your Son gave me when He was nailed to the cross. I know the true sacrifice has already been made for me, but this is my living sacrifice to You. I turn away from my comfort. I lay it at Your feet. I seek forgiveness

for allowing it to hinder the calling You have on my life and ask You to remove any desire to return to that place. In Jesus' name, I pray.

Here are some scriptures and affirmations to help you as you step out of your comfort zone.

SCRIPTURES

Those who belong to Christ Jesus have crucified the flesh with its passions and desires. Galatians 5:24 NIV

Arise, for it is your task, and we are with you; be strong and do it. Ezra 10:4 ESV

Set your minds on things above, not on earthly things Colossians 3:2 NIV

For I know the plans I have for you," declares the LORD, "plans to prosper you and not to harm you, plans to give you hope and a future. Jeremiah 29:11 NIV

When I was a child, I talked like a child, I thought like a child, I reasoned like a child. When I became a man, I put the ways of childhood behind me. 1 Corinthians 13:11 NIV

AFFIRMATIONS

I step out on faith, knowing God is there to catch me.

I say goodbye to things that hinder me from the life I am created for.

Obstacle Three: Fear

When I was younger, I would go with my aunt to sing. It was one of the highlights of my childhood. My aunt knew everybody and she introduced me to so many people. I imagine some days what life would have been like, if I had kept in contact with some of the people I had the privilege of meeting. My aunt was one of those people who never met a stranger. She had this air about her where people seemed excited to just be in her presence. When I was with my aunt, I felt I could do anything. I remember going to a concert with my cousin. She and I had the privilege of opening for a very high profile artist. At the time, I didn't see the significance in knowing this woman or singing for her, but now I can see it was major accomplishment, something I will never forget. There was no fear. We just stood on that stage, waited for my aunt to play that certain key and began to sing. It didn't matter the hundreds of people looking at us. It didn't matter if we happened to sing the wrong note. It didn't matter whether our outfits matched or not. It didn't matter if our hair was perfect. It didn't even matter if they liked what we sung. We were just two girls excited about singing. Fear was nowhere around. Even now I smile thinking about that moment and feel the freedom of no fear.

I also remember as a youth leader taking a group of youth to a retirement home and my pastor at the time asking me to sing a song. I still get teary-eyed and a lump fills my throat when I think about how afraid I was when the words came out of his mouth. I hadn't even gotten to the point of singing when fear took over; it was the mere idea of singing alone in front of people. I was terrified.

I was among people who were highly medicated, some of them didn't even realize we were in the room. The ones who did were just excited to have someone visit them. We could have sung Twinkle, Twinkle Little Star and they would have been happy. However, I remember standing in the floor trembling. My hands were sweaty, my heart was pounding so hard I could feel each beat in my throat and it wasn't the beat to the song I wanted to sing so it was throwing my rhythm off. I was so afraid.

I remember wiping my hands on my jeans as I stood to walk towards the platform. My hands were so sweaty, I left hand prints on my pants. Not only was I afraid, I had two handprints on my jeans. I had a group of youth looking at me as their leader. I had a pastor clearly unaware of how terrified his request made me. I had my husband dealing with his own nervousness as he prepared to speak a word of encouragement to the group. I would have loved for him to have spoken a word of encouragement to me but he was dealing with his own fears. Then I had the ever-ready group of elderly people staring at me. Some were looking at me with great expectations, some were looking at me trying figure out who I was and why I was even there, and the remainder were looking off into space trying figure out why they were there. Clearly, I was not going to get much encouragement from anyone in this group.

It is amazing how two similar, yet different events could provide such drastically different feelings and memories. As children, we tend not to dwell on fear, expectations, or appearances. Until the first encounter with fear, children are fearless and relentless, willing to try anything. But as soon as fear creeps in, life takes a dramatic turn.

It's easy to quote scriptures about fear or give some motivational speech about not giving up. But living through fear is hard. Fear all by itself can leave you paralyzed, unable to move forward and afraid to go back. The fear I felt at the rest home was real. I have yet to stand before a group to sing alone again and that happened over 20 years ago.

Many would tell me to face that fear and go out and sing again. I don't have a desire to sing like that anymore. However, every time I stand before a group to speak, I'm visited by all those emotions and fears. Each time I stand before a group of people, I fight fear: fear of saying the right thing, fear of whether I will be accepted, fear of whether I will be understood, fear of whether I will get my point across, fear of letting myself or someone else down, fear no one will be moved by what I say, even fear of fear! I've learned to push past it, move through it, not allow it to hold me hostage, and to embrace that just like the people in the rest home, someone is just glad that I'm there and talking to them. Even if one person is reached by something I have said, it makes that battle with fear worth it.

Fear is defined by Google as an unpleasant emotion caused by the belief that someone or something is dangerous, likely to cause pain, or a threat. I would like to go deeper and say, fear is the mind's inability to control beliefs, thoughts and/or emotions developed concerning an unknown outcome.

Fear shows up differently for everyone. The same fear that can cause one person to become paralyzed and do absolutely nothing can motivate someone else to do the miraculous. If I haven't learned anything else, facing fears can be difficult, but not impossible. Fear is an emotion and emotions change. When you face a fear, it must respond. It's when you run from your fears, they become bigger than life. They become those things that keep you stuck and unable to do the things you desire.

Fear shows up in many ways. Not only are there psychological or emotional symptoms of fear like anxiety, depression, or stress, but it can also have a physical effect on you. Fear has been known to cause headaches, uncontrollable sweating, rapid heartbeat, shortness of breath, heart attacks, strokes, even death.

Fear can be like heavy weights chained to you. Not only do they weigh you down but they keep you grounded. They keep you from moving forward. Fear prevents you from experiencing the peace that God ordained for you.

When you allow your fears to overwhelm you it prevents you from living the life God created you to live. It's easy to get caught up in your fears, but when your fears begin to hinder you from doing the things that God has placed on your heart to do, it's time to deal with them.

External Fears

There are thousands of fears in the world. Did you know the top fear among women is Arachnophobia, the fear of spiders? I don't have a fear of spiders but I don't go around looking for them either. The fear of spiders falls into a category called external fears. These are fears caused by a specific event or something outside of you. External fears are triggered by certain circumstances.

When I was younger, I taught myself to swim. Well it was more that I taught myself to stay under water long enough to push my body a few feet while flapping my arms and legs. It wasn't anything fancy. I would never win a prize for speed and I definitely wouldn't get a prize for grace. At some moments, I can imagine that I looked like a fish who had been caught on a hook and was desperately trying to get away.

I only used my newly found acrobatic skills on special occasions, like summer vacation with the family. At the time, only my oldest son and I could swim, so we used these moments as our bonding time. We would swim to the other side of the pool, enjoy a brief conversation and wave back at the others sitting on the far side of the pool as if we were talking about them. It was fun and it will always be a part of our memories.

I remember the year I was pregnant with my youngest son. When I went underwater, I almost drowned. No exaggeration! I was gasping for air. If the lifeguard didn't come get me out of the water, I would have probably killed myself with all the extra flapping I was doing. I say that because truth be told, all I had to do was stand up and I would have been fine. But at the time I was drowning and I knew it. You can't tell me any different. It was that specific event that caused me to have a fear of swimming for a long time. It wasn't until my son was in his early teens that I even considered putting my head under water again. External fears are triggered by certain events. The fear only occurs when you remember the event.

Are there external fears that keep you from pursuing your dreams? What are they?

_____
_____
_____
_____
_____

Internal Fears

Similar to external fears are internal fears. These fears are also caused by external factors. They are not always associated with any particular circumstance but can be. Internal fears are: fear of success, fear of failure, fear of rejection, and doubt.

For years, I struggled with hypertension issues. My blood pressure would spike, triggering migraines that lasted for several days at a time. There was a season when I was getting a headache at least once a week because we couldn't get my blood pressure under control. When this finally turned around, my doctor told me that if I continued to manage my blood pressure with exercise and proper eating, she would take me off my blood pressure medication, and I was excited. Sadly, as soon as those words registered in my mind, my eating became out of control and I stopped going to the gym. I could feel my blood pressure rising.

The years of no headaches turned into moments of a slight nagging headache every day. What was going on? Why was this happening? It was the fear of success.

I had been on blood pressure medication for over ten years. I had been morbidly obese for more than that. Here I was taking control of my life and I panicked. What if I could pull this off? Was it possible for me to get off the medication? Was it possible I was taking care of myself and getting results? This felt odd. It was completely out of my norm. I had always put everyone else first. I had always fought for everyone else.

If I did this, I wouldn't have any excuses for not accomplishing anything else I put my mind to. I could no longer use my weight or the headaches as reasons for not doing all the things I've used them as excuses for. I would be able to go on that walk with my friends. I would be able to take that hike. I would be able to travel. I wouldn't be too tired. I could no longer hide behind the mask of my weight. But more than anything I would have to keep succeeding! I was so used to failing, I was afraid to succeed.

Internal fears aren't triggered by events. They are triggered by thoughts inside of us. They come from the unknown. We push back from them because we are afraid of what could happen. We are afraid of what we don't know.

Are you afraid of succeeding or failing? Is that fear holding you hostage? Put a name to it so you can face it.

_____

_____

_____

Subconscious Fears

Subconscious fears are very similar to internal fears. Some researchers even use these terms interchangeably but I find subconscious fears are deeper. Just like the other fears, they can paralyze you, and can keep you from even trying. You avoid the situation at all costs. Subconscious fears derive from our own beliefs. They are not always what someone has told us, sometimes they come from what we have convinced ourselves to be true. Your subconscious fears are where superstitions tend to hide out. Remember as a child hearing if you step on the crack you break your mother's back? Have you ever been mad at your mom, saw the crack and thought about stepping on it? Okay, don't answer that! Subconscious fears are true beliefs that if you do something, something bad is going to happen.

During my moment of denial associated with my people pleasing issue, I really believed if I said no to someone, the earth was going to open and I would fall immediately into hell. Don't judge me! I believed if I didn't help others or tend to their needs, I was sinning. I believed that when I said no, regardless of whether it was an inconvenience to me or not, I was being selfish and would be punished because of my selfishness. Many times, I found myself worn out, bitter, and even angry because I was doing something I didn't want to do but afraid if I didn't I would be punished by God.

I remember when my son first started playing baseball. As long as they had the tee stand in position he would hit the ball into outfield but as soon as they removed the stand he would panic. The pitcher would throw the ball and he would stand there watching the ball go by. One day I asked him why he never swung at the ball. His response shocked me. He said, "Because I'm not going to hit it any way. I would rather not swing and hope to be walked than to swing and strike myself out." I couldn't believe what I was hearing but that's subconscious fear! He believed he would not be able to hit the ball so he didn't even try. Thankfully we helped him work through that fear and he began to swing at the ball. He even made several homerun hits.

All fears are not bad. Some fears are what I call good fears. They may seem confining but they provide you opportunities to explore a different side of you. Good fears are freeing. They allow you to address areas in your life you may have never addressed before. They are there to protect you from danger. Good fears build confidence. They set you apart. They force you to act and not stay stuck in a defeated position. Good fears bring you life, requiring you to live in the moment. Skydiving, pushing through a past failure, walking across a bridge all can be wrapped in fear but how much excitement comes from facing those fears head on?

What fears have you stuck? You don't even attempt them because of something that happened in the past. Are you ready to face them? Can you see how they are hindering you from pursing your dreams?

_____
_____
_____
_____
_____

Overcoming Fear

In order to overcome any fear, you must face it. The longer you allow it to form and sit in your mind, the stronger it becomes and the more of a crippling effect it can have on you. The method used to face your fears will be different for different people and different circumstances. Some fears you must stand up to, face them, and declare victory over them. This is called immediate exposure. If you have a fear of spiders, immediate exposure would be allowing a spider to crawl on your hand or over your body. Immediate exposure for a person with a fear of rejection could be to get a job as a door-to-door salesperson.

Then there are those fears that you must gradually expose yourself to. I'm still gradually exposing myself to some. Gradual exposure is when you take your time and deal with each stage of the fear. Unlike immediate exposure, gradual exposure usually requires someone to help you move forward. With gradual exposure, it's easy to walk away and declare it's too hard. You will need to be completely focused on getting over the fear and unwilling to allow anything or anyone to stop you, but it can be done. If you have a fear of speaking in front of people, gradual exposure would be you speak into a recorder, then to a mirror, then to a group you know until you are comfortable speaking in front of anyone.

Regardless of which method of exposure you use, to overcome any fear you must face it. Facing your fears can be a challenge. But that's why God is here. That's why we ask God to deliver us from them. The enemy uses fear as a weapon against you. He is clearly aware that if he can keep you from accomplishing your goals by inputting situations and circumstances that cause fear to rise up in you, he can prevent you from walking in the calling God has on your life.

Have you ever been afraid of something and once you faced it, you couldn't figure out why you were afraid? Philippians 4:6-7 says, "Be anxious (fearful) for nothing, but in everything by prayer and supplication, with thanksgiving, let your requests be made known to God; and the peace of God, which surpasses all understanding, will guard your heart and mind through Christ Jesus."

Are you ready to let go of the fear? Are you ready to allow God to give you peace about what has you fearful?

1. Face it – Admit you are afraid. There is the misconception that we shouldn't have fears. That bothers me. The Bible says God did not give us a spirit of fear (2 Timothy 1:7). But it didn't say we wouldn't experience it. The scripture is saying fear didn't come from God. There are even times God will allow you to experience circumstances that will force you to face your fears.

2. Is it fact or belief? – Some things in life are to be feared. When someone comes up to you with a gun, you are going to be afraid. If you are facing a sickness, you are going to be afraid. If someone told you there was a robber down the street and you believe it to be true, that's a belief. You don't know if the person down the street is really a robber and you also don't know if they are going to do anything to hurt you. Why are you afraid?

3. Change your mindset. – Fear is as big as you allow it to be. What are you thinking about the situation? Remember fear is an emotion and emotions are feelings. You are in complete control of your emotions. You can decide how you want to feel. When the fear is based off a belief, you decide if you want to believe it. If it's based off a fact, what are you supposed to learn from it?

4. Give it to God! – That's right! Tell God about it. Be honest with Him. We get so distracted with how we are supposed to act, what we are supposed to feel, and how we are supposed to handle everything. Remember "suppose" opens the door to control. But we cannot, will not, should not, be able to handle everything, especially the things we have never experienced. Fear starts in our minds. Get out of your mind and get on your knees.

Are you ready to deal with your fears? Could your fears be the glue holding your mask in place?

PRAYER

God,
Help me identify the fears that are holding me back from accomplishing the things You have for me to do. Your word declares You did not give me a spirit of fear, so I ask You to expose the root of the fear that I may be able to walk according to Your desires for me. God if the fear that I face is to draw me closer to You, I ask You to strengthen me and help me endure. Yet if the fear is formed from beliefs or circumstances outside of Your will, take them away that I might be able to move forward in my calling. God, I don't want anything including fear to stand between us. Help me! In Jesus name, I pray.

Here are some scriptures and affirmations that helped me as I asked God to help me deal with my fears.

SCRIPTURES

So do not fear, for I am with you; do not be dismayed, for I am your God. I will strengthen you and help you; I will uphold you with my righteous right hand. Isaiah 41:10 NIV

When anxiety was great within me, your consolation brought joy to my soul. Psalm 94:19 NIV

The Lord is my light and my salvation—whom shall I fear? The Lord is the stronghold of my life—of whom shall I be afraid? Psalm 27:1 ERV

Be strong and courageous. Do not fear or be in dread of them, for it is the LORD your God who goes with you. He will not leave you or forsake you. Deuteronomy 31:6 NIV

AFFIRMATIONS

I'm conquering my fears one at a time with God's help.
I focus on the truth not my fears.

I am free from any type of fear because greatness dwells in me.

I am willing to try new things courageously.

I courageously challenge the unknown and grow from it.

Surrender

I grew up around boys, boys, and more boys. There were a lot of pranks, horseplay, and wrestling. I can remember my mom constantly telling my brothers not to be so rough with me. It really didn't mean anything to them. In my opinion, that announcement encouraged them to be even rougher. Although it didn't always feel like it when they were dragging me across the floor or throwing me on the bed, I knew my brothers would never hurt me or allow me to be hurt. They even created a system to reassure me. The system consisted of me tapping three times on the floor, which I'm sure they got from all the wrestling shows they watched. If I tapped, the horseplay stopped immediately. I tapped out a lot!

Funny how I never remember them tapping out for me. Although they were bigger and stronger, I'm sure I had some pretty good moves in there at some point. I think I'll demand a rematch!

My tapping out was an indication of my surrender. It meant I was done. It meant they had won. It meant I didn't want to play anymore. And many times, it meant I felt defeated and was about to get mad. I did that a lot. If I couldn't win, I would get mad, storm off and pout, which resulted in them getting in trouble. I always wondered why my brothers would allow it to get that far but today I can say it was those moments of horseplay that taught me to defend myself. Those moments helped me to fight through some tough situations. Those moments built my strength.

Growing up surrendering always meant giving up! It was acknowledging someone was better or more powerful than you. Surrendering was a sign of weakness. Surrendering was the last result. Surrendering was the end all. It meant you were out of the game. I was trained early that you didn't surrender unless it was absolutely necessary. I held onto these lessons, and brought them into my adult life.

- You don't give up unless absolutely necessary.
- You don't quit!
- You don't let anyone get the best of you.
- You stand firm.
- Most important, you never let them see you sweat!

Do not surrender because you lose! It was so bad I even used misinterpreted scripture to back up my belief. "I can do all things through Christ who strengthens me" (Philippians 4:13). The part I didn't take into consideration when quoting that scripture which I found was the most important part – through Christ!

My strength or what I found to be the lack thereof was not my own doing. In fact, I soon learned I was extremely weak by myself. But in my weakness, God would prove to be very strong (2 Corinthians 12:9). That took years for me to learn.

It wasn't until I learned the true definition of surrender and asked for help that I was able to get rid of my need to have things my way. It wasn't until I learned that my weakness was really strength that I grew in my faith.

Did it happen overnight? No way! In fact, I'm still fighting some of those battles. But I will say, surrendering helped me identify my purpose. It grew my confidence. It showed me who I was and whose I was. It helped me see past the surface of things and dig deeper to get a clear understanding of why things are happening the way they are.

I realized quickly it wasn't about how great I am but it's about the greatness that dwells inside of me.

I believe one of the reasons we struggle with surrendering is because we don't quite understand what it means. Like I said for years I thought it was the worst thing a person could ever do. It wasn't until I truly came to a point where I had to surrender, you know that "last resort" type deal, that I realized it was for my own benefit that I did.

Let's look at what surrendering is and what it's not.

Surrendering IS

Surrendering is to stop hiding. When you surrender, you take off the mask and give what's behind it to God to heal. Surrendering is to stop fighting. Surrendering is letting go of the need to fight life and what is happening. We go through many of our struggles because we refuse to learn the lessons they are teaching us.

Surrendering is to stop resisting. Surrendering helps us to comply with the powers that be. Not in a demeaning or belittling way but in an authoritative way. We are saying okay, let's see what you are working with.

Surrendering is to subject your thoughts, will, and desires over to something bigger than you. Let's make this clear, unlike surrendering in the world, when you surrender to God, you allow Him to guide your thoughts, your will, and your desires.

Surrendering is to give up your willpower and subject it to something greater. Giving up your willpower can be very scary. I mean, all I have is my willpower. If I give that away what's left? God is not asking you to become nonexistent without thoughts or feelings. He wants you to stop fighting Him. He wants you to find your true power through Him.

Surrendering is a voluntary submission to a better way of doing things. The thing I love about God's request for us to surrender to Him is it's not a mandate. You don't have to do it. You can live your life any way you desire. You can have it your way, but you must also deal with the consequences that come along with having your way.

Surrendering is willingly realizing you don't have all the answers. I consider myself a pretty smart person as should you, but I had to realize I didn't have all the answers. If I had all the answers, I probably would not find myself in some of the situations that needed God's intervention.

Surrendering is accepting the way you have been doing things isn't working and being willing to try something different. There were some areas in my life I quickly turned over to God after realizing I couldn't fix them. Then there are those areas in my life I tend to keep holding on to. I will ask Him to help me but I won't follow His instructions.

Surrendering is NOT

Surrendering is NOT laying down and being mistreated. You were not created to do that! No one has the right to mistreat or misuse you. God never intended you to live a life like that.

Surrendering is NOT a show of weakness. Quite the contrary! To truly surrender takes strength and a lot of it. To stop fighting for what you've believed in in lieu of something that "may" be better takes a lot of strength.

Surrendering is NOT for the cowardly. A coward is a person who lacks courage to do or endure dangerous or unpleasant things (Oxford Press). Surrendering will cause you to go through some unpleasant situations. It will cause you to dig deep inside to find strength you didn't know you had.

Surrendering is NOT saying no to what you want. When you really surrender your will over to God, you are saying yes to the desires of your heart because now they will line up with what He has for you, not the mediocre thoughts or dreams that you have for yourself.

Surrendering is NOT failure. The world will tell you surrendering is a sign of failure, but how can you fail with God? How can you fail doing things His way? Remember He created you and knows the end of the story.

Surrendering is NOT because of fear. God does not want you to fear Him. He wants you to trust Him. You are never required to surrender because of fear. It is VOLUNTARY!

How to surrender

There is no magical process you go through to surrender. You decide! Will it happen overnight? It didn't for me. It took time. It took trial and error. It took perseverance. It took hitting rock bottom. Yep, you read that right! I didn't truly surrender until I hit rock bottom.

In fact, it took me hitting rock bottom a few times.

I remember vividly the night I cried out to God and asked Him to please deliver me from me. Deliver me from my fears. Deliver me from my need to control. Deliver me from my comfort of being miserable. Deliver me. Please deliver me. I could tell you everything that was transpiring in my life but it doesn't matter. What matters is, I was broken. I was hurt. I was lost. I was lonely. I was depressed. I didn't know who to turn to. I didn't know what to do. Everything in my life that I had cherished and sacrificed for appeared to be slipping through my hands and I could not stop it. It was one of the scariest moments in my life, but it was a moment that changed my life forever. It is my prayer that you don't have to experience a moment like that. But if you do, remember God loves you and He will bring through it.

What does it feel like?

    Surrendering feels like peace. Have you ever been in a situation and everyone around you is upset or angry? The situation is out of control. You should be upset but you are not. That's what surrendering feels like. You truly trust God to fix the situation. It does NOT mean there is no situation, you just don't let it control your emotions.

    The need to manipulate others to get what you want, no longer exists. Forcing people to see your point of view becomes no longer important. The need to be in control seems pointless and impossible, but you are okay with it. I was excited when someone else took control of the situation. It allowed me time to focus on things I could control and things I enjoyed doing.

    Here is the thing. Most of us are willing to surrender if it means we are going to get something in return. But what if God does not answer the prayer the way you expected? What if He does not heal the loved one? What if the marriage ends in divorce? What if the child does not get saved? What if you lose the job? What if… are you still willing to surrender? Are you still willing to let go of your way of doing things? Are you willing to be quiet when you want to yell? Are you willing to sit still when you want to fight?

    Are you willing to allow God to fight the battle for you? Are you willing to wait for instructions on how to proceed? Are you willing to walk away from the job? Are you ready to stop lying to get your way? Are you ready to let the other person be right? Are you ready to listen to people talk about you and say nothing to defend yourself?

Are you willing to be lied on? Are you willing to be told what you should do by people who don't know your situation? Are you ready for people you thought would always be there to walk away because they don't understand what you are doing? Are you willing to let God's way be THE WAY?

If you are ready to say yes, go forward to the prayer of surrender. If you feel this is too drastic and you aren't quite ready, let's pray that God prepares you by showing you the areas in your life where surrendering has caused you pain.

I need to surrender
1. _____
2. _____
3. _____

Now that you understand why it could be hard for you to surrender, I have a question for you. How has holding onto that pain helped you? Do you find yourself constantly battling the repercussions associated with those decisions to hold on? Is that pain something you are hiding behind your mask? When was the last time you found peace in those areas?

When you are ready to surrender it to God, the prayer of Surrender will be here for you!

Prayer of Surrender

God,

Thank you that regardless of what I have done in the past, You are willing to forgive and allow me a chance to lay it at Your feet. Thank You that I can surrender the issues that I've hidden behind my mask without fear of them being thrown back in my face. Thank You for helping me walk away from those issues and remove the desire for them. Thank You that even though I don't how I'm going to live without the issues I've hidden behind my mask, I can trust that You will help me. Thank You that should I desire to pick them back up, You will be there to guide me away from them. Thank You that my past is my past and I can walk in my new creation. God, when the enemy tries to throw in my face the person I was prior to praying this prayer, help me to remember you have already accepted my request for forgiveness, forgave me, and delivered me from it. In Jesus' name, I pray - AMEN!

ABOUT THE AUTHOR

Tina Bailey is a certified Christian Life Coach and transformational speaker. She empowers women daily with encouragement, support, and words of wisdom through social media and her personal blog.

As a survivor of domestic abuse, Tina was determined to find ways to bring the help she desperately needed to others in a similar situation. Her efforts birthed what is now

The H.E.L.P. Conference. This is an annual conference that provides resources and encouragement to women from all walks of life. Believing your past does not determine your destiny, she has devoted her life to helping women believe this as well.

In her free time, Tina enjoys blogging and spending time with her 5 "young adult children" and her grandson.

www.ingramcontent.com/pod-product-compliance
Lightning Source LLC
Chambersburg PA
CBHW070550300426
44113CB00011B/1850